# I Like Pasta

By Jennifer Julius

Welcome
**Books**

Children's Press
A Division of Grolier Publishing
New York / London / Hong Kong / Sydney
Danbury, Connecticut

Photo Credits: Cover, 5, 7, 9, 11, 13, 15, 17, 21 by Maura Boruchow; p. 19 © IndexStock Photography, Inc.

Contributing Editor: Jennifer Ceaser
Book Design: Nelson Sa

Library of Congress Cataloging-in-Publication Data

Julius, Jennifer.
　I like pasta / by Jennifer Julius.
　　p. cm. — (Good food)
　Includes bibliographical references and index.
　ISBN 0-516-23132-4 (lib. bdg.) — ISBN 0-516-23057-3 (pbk.)
　1. Cookery (Pasta)—Juvenile literature. [1. Pasta products.] I. Title. II. Series.

　TX809.M17 J85 2000
　641.8′22—dc21

00-043067

# Contents

I like pasta.

Do you like pasta?

Pasta comes in all shapes and sizes.

This pasta is long and thin.

It looks like strings.

It is spaghetti (speh-**geh**-tee).

This pasta is square.

It is filled with cheese.

It is ravioli (ra-vee-**oh**-lee).

9

This pasta is **flat**.

The edges are **wavy**.

It is lasagna (leh-**zah**-nyah).

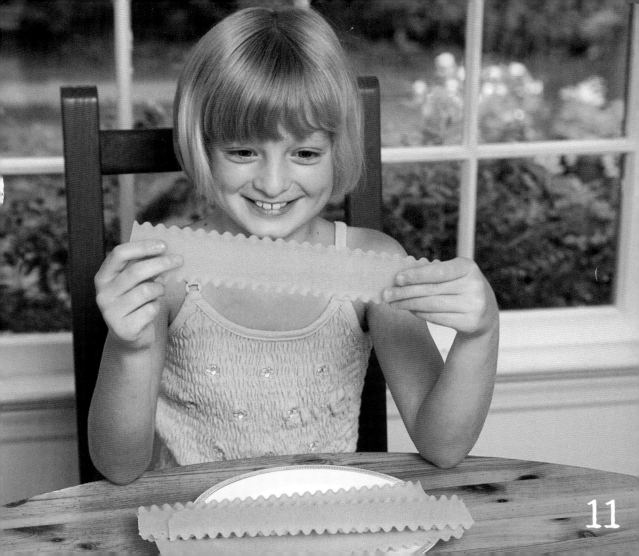

This pasta is shaped like an **elbow**.

I eat it with cheese.

It is macaroni (mak-eh-**roh**-nee).

13

This pasta looks like a butterfly.

It is bow tie pasta!

This pasta is shaped like a shell.

It has cheese inside.

I eat the pasta with tomato **sauce**.

All pasta is made from **dough**.

Flour, salt, and eggs make dough.

19

What kind of pasta do you like to eat?

# New Words

dough (**doh**) a mix of flour, salt, and eggs

elbow (**el**-boh) the part of your body where your arm bends

flat (**flat**) smooth and even

sauce (**saws**) something poured over food

wavy (**way**-vee) bending like a wave